PRACTICAL STUFF FOR PASTORS

TAKING CARE OF BUSINESS

Loveland, CO

Real. **Bold.** Love.

Group resources actually work!

This Group resource incorporates our R.E.A.L. approach to ministry. It reinforces a growing friendship with Jesus, encourages long-term learning, and results in life transformation, because it's

Relational
Learner-to-learner interaction enhances learning and builds Christian friendships.

Experiential
What learners experience through discussion and action sticks with them up to 9 times longer than what they simply hear or read.

Applicable
The aim of Christian education is to equip learners to be both hearers and doers of God's Word.

Learner-based
Learners understand and retain more when the learning process takes into consideration how they learn best.

PRACTICAL STUFF FOR PASTORS:
TAKING CARE OF BUSINESS

Visit our website: **group.com**

Credits
Editor: Rick Edwards
Assistant Editors: Kelsey Perry, Ardeth Carlson
Art and Design: Amy Taylor, Andy Towler, Darrin Stoll
Contributing Authors: Tom Barnes, Rick Edwards, Rusty Fulling, Mark Lail, Tony Myles, Larry Shallenberger, Lynne Steckelberg, Brian Walton

Unless otherwise indicated, all Scripture quotations are taken from the *Holy Bible*, New Living Translation, copyright © 1996, 2004, 2007, 2013 by Tyndale House Foundation. Used by permission of Tyndale House Publishers, Inc., Carol Stream, Illinois 60188. All rights reserved.

ISBN 978-1-4707-2328-6

Printed in the United States of America.

10 9 8 7 6 5 4 3 2 1   24 23 22 21 20 19 18 17 16 15

CONTENTS

INTRODUCTION

When we at Group Publishing wondered what kind of resource we could offer to pastors, we asked hundreds of pastors what they wish they'd learned in seminary but didn't. The overwhelming response was "practical stuff." This book is our response.

However, if you need to fix the leaky faucet in the first floor ladies' room, Google it. This book isn't *that* practical.

If you want to know the best accounting practices to prepare for an IRS audit of a 501(c) (3) nonprofit religious organization, consult a tax lawyer. We didn't have enough pages to cover such a complicated subject.

And if you are looking for the perfect volume setting on the sanctuary sound system that satisfies everyone…well, we all know that book will never be written.

Practical Stuff for Pastors is a series of handbooks dedicated to topics such as how to manage a team, handle property and financial issues, diffuse conflicts, lead change, and more. We've assembled a team of pastors, church leaders, and business professionals who provide tips, recommendations, and strategies for the practical responsibilities pastors deal with on a regular basis.

In keeping with this book's practical approach, you'll find that the table of contents doubles as a topical index. The plain, straightforward chapter titles don't try to be clever but clearly describe the topic they address. The stand-alone chapters can be read in any sequence, at any time you need to access them. The writing style is informal, with easy, accessible language. (And we used mostly short words!)

So whenever you need to look up how to do some practical ministry stuff:

- Look up your topic in the table of contents.
- Read the chapter.
- Act on what you read: make a call, plan a meeting, create a job description, or delegate a task.

Taking Care of Business

This volume of Practical Stuff for Pastors focuses on the business of the church—the administration of people, money, buildings, resources, and all the other nitty-gritty details that pastors are charged with overseeing.

As noted in the chapter on church budgets, matters of resource administration, including money management, might not seem to be very spiritual. Churches, and pastors in particular, may be reluctant to immerse themselves in such worldly concerns. Thankfully, though, God did not think our world was too dirty to dive headlong into it in the person of Jesus Christ. If we follow that pattern, we will find that any aspect of human existence can be reclaimed for the sake of God's kingdom—including church administration.

Of course, the opposite approach can also negatively affect the church. When taken to an extreme, the business model can overshadow or ignore the divine nature and mission of the church. Growth strategies, leadership principles, real estate deals, and complicated financial practices may receive the lion's share of the staff's time and attention. This might be especially true of megachurches (and those of any size that aspire to become a megachurch).

Nathaniel Tate, administrator of Potter's House church in Dallas, Texas (T.D. Jakes, pastor), identifies a good balance between the spiritual and mundane nature of church administration:

"While the church is an organism—a living, breathing thing established by God and left to affect this world— it still must be organized in order to be completely effective and maintain integrity in business. The administrator should have the business savvy to deal with the complex nature of the 21st-century church."[1]

This handbook is designed to help you become a little more savvy about human resources, money management, building projects, and other business-related topics. The chapters are not exhaustive treatments, but they should at least ground you in the basics and point you to resources for further investigation. May this humble handbook be a useful guide for those times you are called to administer some of God's many gifts to the church.

"Now you are Christ's body, and individually members of it. And God has appointed in the church...gifts of...administrations."

— 1 Corinthians 12:27-28,
New American Standard Bible

SAFETY AND RISK MANAGEMENT

Most pastors view risk management as a necessary evil, a formidable task that gets between them and the ministry they would rather be doing. The prospect of sitting in endless meetings to crank out boilerplate policies instead of actually doing ministry is demotivating. Part of the problem comes in pitting the task of risk management against "real" ministry.

The term "risk management" comes to the church from the legal and insurance worlds, so it isn't a particularly spiritual term. But it goes far beyond creating binders full of policies and procedures. The goal of risk management is to create a culture that protects and cares for the staff, congregation, properties, and ministry of the church. This culture will thrive only when widespread buy-in occurs. Pastors and church leaders can help their congregations (and themselves) appreciate the importance of risk management by using biblical terms such as "stewardship" (Genesis 1:28) and "shepherding" (1 Peter 5:2-4). Seen in this light, protecting God's people is a central part of ministry.

"Care for the flock that God has entrusted to you. Watch over it willingly, not grudgingly—not for what you will get out of it, but because you are eager to serve God."

—1 Peter 5:2

Who Manages Risk

The ultimate responsibility for overseeing your church's risk management strategy falls to the governing board of your church. Meanwhile, staff members should be made responsible for identifying the best practices over their departments and implementing them. From there, ownership works its way into the volunteers as staff members lead their respective teams.

You can use this process to strengthen your church's ability to steward and shepherd the congregation:

1. Identify and assess all the risks your church currently faces. Estimate the likelihood of those risks occurring and the severity of the consequence that comes with each risk. (Note: Some team members may try to minimize the likelihood of certain risks with a "that could never happen here" attitude. Combat this lazy and naïve perspective by having on hand the best data available. Your insurance carrier should be able to help you with this.)

2. Prioritize your list of risks, from the most detrimental to the least detrimental.

3. Determine which of the known risks have been addressed.

4. Reduce the identified risks as much as reasonably possible.

5. Repeat this exercise on an annual basis.

Touch Points to Consider

As you, your boards, and staff work together to identify the risks threatening your church, consider the following.

- Can your corporate structure be altered in a way that reduces the liability of the whole church? For example, if your church operates a day care center, could you establish it as its own legal entity to help protect the church in the event of a lawsuit?

- Are your policy and procedure manuals up-to-date and comprehensive? Do they reflect current legal and ethical rules? Make it a practice to annually "audit" these guiding documents and promptly revise them as needed.

- Does the way your church *actually* operates match your constitution, bylaws, manuals, and other official documents? A discrepancy can open your church up to a lawsuit. For example, if an individual is guilty of immoral behavior and is removed from membership in a manner not prescribed by your governing documents, that person could initiate a costly and embarrassing lawsuit. Additionally, you need to make sure your documents address all necessary provisions, as well. Using the same example as above, removing someone from membership without having any provision at all for such an event also opens the door to litigation.

- Do you have systems in place to make sure the offering money is securely taken and deposited? Are there systems in place to discourage the embezzlement of funds?

  For more details on budgets and money management, see the "Creating and Managing Church Budgets" chapter in this book, as well as "Handling Financial Conflicts" in *Practical Stuff for Pastors: Dealing With Conflict.*

- Has your church secured its tax-exempt status, and is your church in compliance with the regulations that come with it? The IRS website has a page of helpful information for churches to better understand these laws.[2]

- Is your church's insurance coverage adequate? You'll need insurance for property and casualty, employee theft, general liability, sexual misconduct (including sexual molestation), and director and officer liability. Do you have insurance to handle lawsuits related to employment practices such as discrimination claims, wrongful termination, or sexual harassment? Some churches carry "key man" liability to guard themselves from the financial losses that might come from losing a prominent leader, such as a popular pastor.

- Does your church have a human resource manual that outlines the professional and moral expectations of its staff?

For more details on staff administration, see the "Day-to-Day Administration" chapter in this book.

- Does your church observe current best practices for child protection? Churches have a special responsibility to protect their children. Jesus elevated the value of children and warned those who would harm them (Matthew 18:1-6). High-profile news stories have documented how devastating a case of child molestation is for the victims and their families, as well as the church or nonprofit that employed the offender. A church and its leadership can quickly find its reputation and financial position damaged for years. Study the best practices for child protection, and stay current on the published literature on the topic.

- What are your church's emergency response plans? Do you have a plan for safely evacuating the building during a fire? Or where to safely hunker down during a severe storm or tornado? What is the protocol for responding to someone experiencing a medical crisis? If services or meetings are canceled due to inclement weather or other events, do you have a system for rapid communication to the congregation (for example, phone "calling trees" or email or text alerts)?

- Do you have a public-relations policy for dealing with a publicized crisis? In the event of a crisis, only church-approved spokespersons should address the media. This allows the church to present an accurate and consistent message about the circumstance and how the church is responding to it.

- What is your plan to keep your building well maintained to prevent unnecessary injury? In colder climates, you need a plan for removing snow from parking lots and sidewalks. Electrical and plumbing systems, fire and smoke alarms, and suppression systems should be inspected regularly. Kitchen equipment and facilities need to be maintained and regularly checked, too.

- Does your church have a plan for leadership succession if the senior pastor were to resign? Many churches suffer a loss of momentum and reduced attendance and giving after a founding or long-tenured leader steps down. The average search for a new senior pastor takes 18 to 24 months, which is enough time for the church to experience lasting damage.

Tapping Into Existing Expertise

The above list will get you started on the right path to identify and reduce risk. Even though this list is hardly complete, the prospect of becoming familiar with each of these arenas does seem exhausting. But remember that you're working with a team of staff and/or volunteers. Delegate responsibility to the appropriate board or staff members. Point them to the right literature, resources, and mentors, and expect them to become knowledgeable in their areas. Then encourage them to connect with the knowledge base already in your congregation, such as insurance agents, attorneys, doctors, social workers, teachers, and law enforcement officers. These professionals will have the expertise your church needs. You'll quickly become a team of stewards and shepherds working together to protect your congregation.

By Larry Shallenberger

DAY-TO-DAY ADMINISTRATION

Have you seen this before? An eager new children's ministry coordinator who oozes a passion for Jesus and kids joins your ministry. Initially he fits in quite nicely. However, within two years he has left. Later you hear through the grapevine that he's out of ministry altogether, happily ensconced in an entirely new career field. What went wrong?

According to the Mayo Clinic, three of the factors leading to job burnout are lack of control, unclear job expectations, and work–life imbalance.[3] You can go a long way toward remedying all three of these factors by focusing on the day-to-day administration of your ministry.

How do you manage the day-to-day administration to avoid burnout and keep your employees refreshed and engaged? Be sure employees clearly understand their job responsibilities, and encourage healthy boundaries between work time and personal life. Mixing care and compassion for your employees with knowledge of the legal requirements for your church will create a healthy environment for a thriving ministry.

Fair Labor Standards Act (FLSA)

Churches in the U.S. need to know about the Fair Labor Standards Act. This federal law mandates minimum-wage and overtime rules for organizations as well as individuals. Most churches are not accountable to the FLSA because they don't regularly engage in interstate commerce. But many churches could be, and an individual employee might be covered due to specific duties. Having a preschool on site may mean your church engages in commerce, so the preschool employees would be covered by FLSA. A church that sells a book in another state might have employees covered by FLSA. To avoid breaking federal laws, learn about your compliance requirements, with the advice of an attorney or certified public accountant.

Giving Employees Control

In ministry, most employees "work" on Sunday and take off some other weekday. Based on your coverage under FLSA (see sidebar above), you may have exempt (salaried) and nonexempt (hourly) employees (see sidebar on facing page). Whether or not FLSA overtime pay is required, it's a good idea to manage time within the designated work week to avoid burnout. Allow as much flexibility as you can in scheduling work hours, while balancing out legal requirements. Hourly employees should aim for a 40-hour work week to avoid possible overtime requirements and, more importantly, to manage work–life balance! Be flexible and balanced within each work week. For example, if a Saturday event requires an employee to work 8 hours, have that person take off 8 hours on the Friday before.

Exempt employees (salaried) do not have the same requirements for minimum wage and overtime payments, but they do have a minimum weekly salary requirement. In order to be classified as exempt, they must be an executive, administrative, professional, outside sales, or computer employee, according to their actual job duties.[4] The U.S. Department of Labor regulates these requirements, and your state may have requirements, as well.

Clergy are usually exempt employees (salaried) because they are in a traditional learned profession that requires specialized education. The work is intellectual and requires exercising discretion and judgment. Taxation for clergy can be extremely complex. A good tax accountant and IRS Publication 517 are great resources for learning more about taxation for clergy and religious workers.

If your nonexempt employees (hourly) are covered by the FLSA as described in the previous sidebar, you will need to be aware of requirements concerning minimum wage, overtime, recordkeeping, and youth employment requirements.

DAY-TO-DAY ADMINISTRATION

Another way to give employees control is through a paid-time-off policy, including vacation and sick time. Paid time off can be expensive for a church, but it will help you retain employees by allowing them to re-energize and to care for personal obligations. Paid time off can include both vacation hours and sick hours. Another form of paid time off makes no distinction between sick and vacation time; how it is used is up to the employee. When setting up your paid-leave policy, check state and federal requirements regarding termination pay; requirements for paying unused paid time off vary.

Consider unpaid leave, as well. You could create an unpaid-leave policy unique to your church, such as a six-week personal-leave policy. Larger U.S. organizations are required to follow the Family and Medical Leave Act.

Once you have some rules in place, how do you track employee time worked and days off? Start with the financial software used for the organization. Simply add a time and attendance or payroll module to that system. Or track worked time using a paper form or Excel spreadsheet. Often exempt employees track exceptions only, such as paid time off (or unpaid leave, if it is available).

Clarifying Job Expectations

All job descriptions should provide individual employees a clear idea of what their job entails. Day-to-day expectations for the church as a whole can be defined and clarified in an employee handbook. A badly written handbook could actually increase a church's liability, so take care in creating such a handbook. For example, if the handbook states the discipline policy will include one verbal warning and two written warnings before termination and that process isn't followed, the organization has more liability than if they didn't have a handbook. Nevertheless, the benefits of having clearly defined expectations outweigh that risk. With some thought and legal guidance, a handbook can be clear and concise while decreasing liability.

Topics in a church policy handbook could include:

- Ministry history, goals, and mission statement: a glimpse into organizational culture.

- Disclaimers: defining what the handbook is and isn't.

- Definitions and schedules: employee status and classification, hours of operation, workweeks, and paydays.

- General policies and procedures: paid-time-off and unpaid-leave policies, disciplinary policies, and grievance procedures.

- Federal, state, and local employment laws, policies, and required postings.

- Employee benefits: how to share the perks.

Here are a few sources for employee handbook templates and requirements:

- The Society for Human Resource Management (shrm.org)

- The United States Department of Labor (dol.gov)

- National Federation of Independent Business (nfib.com)

Encouraging Work–Life Balance

"Work hard, play hard" may be a cliché, but it's a good concept to keep in mind when encouraging employees to keep a good balance between time spent at work and personal time. God clearly gives gifts to individuals who serve in ministry, in all aspects of ministry. God also set aside the seventh day for complete rest, a holy day, after the six days allowed for ordinary work. The punishment for breaking that rule was death—a rather strong hint that a day of rest was important to God! Encourage your employees to rest, even when they are on fire for their ministry.

What about those employees who work for your organization and volunteer, as well? Whenever employees are doing job-related activities, it likely is work time, even if it is outside their normal schedule. If the church administrative assistant is serving on a

Sunday doing work that is in her job description or a part of her weekday duties, it should be recorded and paid appropriately. Likewise, work done by hourly employees at home or even "voluntarily" could be considered compensable if it is a job-related activity. Good job descriptions—for both hourly and salaried employees—should define which tasks and hours are part of their job and which are truly volunteer. For hourly employees, describe what hours they should be paid for and at what rate if overtime is involved.

Balancing care for your employees and your ministry while following legal requirements can be tricky. The keys are consistency, clarity, and fairness. Make sure you are applying your ministry requirements consistently for all employees. Day-to-day expectations should be communicated to all of your employees by the highest leaders of your local church. If they aren't, employees won't believe, trust, or follow them. Insist (in a firm but loving way) that the administrative assistant take a vacation. Require the youth pastor to limit his work to a set number of hours per week. Encourage a custodian to engage in an outside service opportunity by allowing a flexible schedule. Model these practices yourself. The ideas and administrative tools described here will help your team members retain the enthusiasm they had when first starting their ministry with you.

By Lynne Steckelberg

DAY-TO-DAY ADMINISTRATION

CREATING AND MANAGING CHURCH BUDGETS

Mention the word "budget" to a gathering of pastors and you can just about count on an 80 percent glazed-eye response. Pastoral leadership was supposed to focus on providing their flocks with inspirational preaching, theological depth, spiritual vitality, and dynamic leadership, not numbers on a spreadsheet. However, there is no escaping the power of money in ministry.

Why Budgets Are Important

In any organization, money is allocated according to the priorities established by the leadership. Those priorities reflect an organization's vision, mission, values, and goals. If any organization ought to be concerned with mission and vision, it's the church. So knowing how to create and manage a budget is a necessary part of

> A budget is a necessary part of enabling your church's ministries and keeping them focused on the mission and vision of your church.

enabling your church's ministries and keeping them focused on the mission and vision of your church.

Churches must not fear budgets because they seem "unspiritual." The doctrine of the Incarnation tells us that God's divine mission of redemption took on human flesh in the person of Jesus of Nazareth. Likewise, one way a church's divinely-inspired mission becomes visible is in the annual budget. Rusty Fulling, founder of Fulling Management & Accounting, Inc., works with both for-profit and nonprofit organizations (and is himself a 20-year-veteran church treasurer). He has found that financially successful churches follow good business strategies and practices when creating and managing their budgets.

Who Creates a Budget

Unlike a business, a church cannot raise ticket prices or sell more seats in order to raise revenue or balance a budget. But church leaders *can* implement proven business practices to create a usable budget. For example, the people leading the budget process should include three types of people also found in successful businesses.[5]

Visionary: If the mission and vision of the church set the priorities for the budget, then the vision leader must be involved in creating that budget. In most churches, that person is the lead pastor. Lead pastors don't need to get caught up in all the details of managing the budget, but they should at least know where the money is supposed to go and be confident that money is indeed being spent according to the approved budget.

Manager: The church treasurer operates as budget manager. This does not mean they alone are in charge of the church's purse strings, even if money gets tight. (Note to church treasurers: It's not your money!) Everyone—including pastor, treasurer, and department heads—should share the load for developing and managing the budget. The treasurer's role is to put together a simple financial report reflecting expected income minus anticipated expenses. Once the budget is approved, the treasurer should provide each ministry/department a monthly report of its income and expenses compared to the original budget.

Technician: Children's pastors, music/worship directors, outreach ministers, and other department heads who oversee individual ministries all fall under the category of technician. Each department head should submit a budget based on ministry needs for the upcoming year. Once their budgets have been approved, the department heads should make sure their income and expenses are within their budgets each month.

How to Create a Budget

When church leaders create a budget, they can follow the same basic steps that for-profit businesses do when they look at factors such as sales cycles, return on investment, and number of customers. There are a number of corresponding practices that churches should follow.

1. Assess your mission and values; then prioritize. Budgets should reflect your philosophy of ministry, not drive it. Allocation of money is directly linked to your values and goals.

2. Review historical trends on all spending areas and income patterns. Compare those to other churches your size.

3. Evaluate the results of last year's ministries and events relative to their expenses.

4. Assign specific numbers to the major expense categories:

   - *Fixed costs:* Costs such as mortgage payments, staff salaries, and utilities are pretty much the same each month, every month.

   - *Variable costs:* Transportation (fuel), food, office supplies, and curriculum and other educational materials are costs you know you will incur. The timing and amounts are less predictable than fixed costs. These costs are often a guesstimate, so aim a little high.

- *One-time costs:* Some one-time expenses may be predictable, such as a new bulb for that projector that's been looking a bit dim lately or the annual Easter egg hunt. Others may be unpredictable, such as broken water pipes. Predict as best you can, and then pad the budget for unexpected emergencies.

5. Develop monthly budgets based on a calendar of events and seasonal swings:

- December's income may be higher than other months due to year-end giving.

- June and July income may be less than other months due to members' summer vacations.

- Summer and early fall expenses may be higher due to VBS programs and ministries based on school-year calendars (children's and youth ministries, for example).

6. Study and adjust to church demographics that influence the budget:

- Define giving units: How many people give $1,000+, $5,000+, $10,000+ each year?

- Age of giving units.

- Number of weekly attendees.

7. Add the numbers to check that they are realistic, making sure your income covers your expenses. Adjust income and/or expense expectations accordingly.

The final product should be as comprehensive as possible but not overly complicated. You should not need a master's degree in accounting to put together and read a budget. Keep it simple. The budget should be able to be read and understood by any of your church members (and they should be welcome to do so).

Managing a Budget

Mission and vision drives the budget planning process. But once in place, your budget can guide and control the ministry. This will help prevent mission "drift" and vision "leakage." Using the budget, rather than filing it away in some drawer for a year, can maintain the focus and effectiveness of all your church's ministries. However, you will need to give daily attention to your finances or they will snowball and bury your ministry.

Even with careful research and planning, budget shortfalls can occur unexpectedly. A sudden sound board failure or a major donor moving away can cause major disruptions to your perfectly prepared budget. Here are a few tactics for tackling a budget shortfall:

- Identify what has caused the shortfall. Is it a one-time issue or an ongoing challenge (such as a deteriorating parking lot or financially undisciplined staff member)?

- Adjust budgets with the input of those directly affected. Be flexible where possible—although some budgets, such as a mortgage, can't be cut.

- Communicate to the entire church. Don't delay, sugarcoat, or hide major shortfalls. Some teams or persons may be important enough that small-group or individual conversations are justified; depending on the cause or need, some donor or groups of donors may be willing to cover the shortfall.

Budgets don't have to be soul-draining or complicated; they can be your friend. All you need is a clear mission and vision plus a committed team of visionaries, managers, and technicians. The resulting budget will guide and enable vital, sustainable ministry year after year.

For leaders without financial expertise, Rusty Fulling recommends *Financial Intelligence: A Manager's Guide to Knowing What the Numbers Really Mean* (Harvard Business School Publishing). Amazon.com quotes *Inc.* magazine in calling it one of "the best, clearest guides to the numbers" on the market.

By Rick Edwards and Rusty Fulling

NAVIGATING THE COMPLEXITIES OF DESIGNATED GIVING

Imagine that a church member informs you he would like to give the church $1 million immediately. Everyone is delighted that God inspired this donor to give to your ministry. Now imagine that the donor has a particular passion for lost people and designates that the funds "be used for evangelism." This condition is certainly within the vision and mission of the church, so you prepare to celebrate. Now imagine that the donor restricts the gift even further: "to provide evangelists to accompany teams exploring the North Pole." A gift so restricted would be practically useless for most churches.

Most donations to churches are unconditional and without designation by the donor. This makes sense theologically: God loves people unconditionally, and in response, people offer unconditional gifts. Sometimes, though, donors give with a bit of instruction, directive, or suggestion. A directive could be due to the nature of the appeal. If a church says "please give to the building fund," they have asked that a particular vision be funded.

However, if God plucks a donor's heartstrings, he or she may give in order to fulfill a personal passion. If a donor has a "burden" for children's ministry, he or she might donate toward the hiring of a children's pastor. All is legitimate and well with designated gifts, provided that the vision of the donor and the vision of the church are in harmony and that the donor gives with no strings attached.

Accounting for Designated Gifts

Some designated gifts are in the form of written documents, and others are simply oral statements. In either case, these gifts would be called a restricted asset. They should be recorded separately in the church's financial records and distinguished from the unrestricted assets (gifts that have no donor-imposed restrictions).

Designated gifts are as diverse as donors, so every church or ministry ought to have a gift-acceptance policy. It should describe what types of designated gifts will be accepted and define how willing the church is to fulfill the donor's wishes. The policy should state that the church will receive only gifts designated for purposes that match the church's purpose and vision. This policy should be clearly stated and widely publicized in the congregation.

Designated gifts are as diverse as donors, so every church or ministry ought to have a gift-acceptance policy.

Responding to Mismatched Gifts

In most cases, it will be immediately clear when a designated gift is not a good fit for the local church. For example, if a church in Florida is offered a sizable sum of money designated for snow and ice removal, there is an opportunity to work with the donor. It would be wise for the donor to either remove the gift's restriction or redirect it to a church where there is measurable annual snowfall.

Whenever possible, try to offer an acceptable alternative that finds common ground between the vision of the church and the heart of the donor. A generous senior adult lady in a church I once pastored wished to make a nice donation in memory of her late husband. Thoughtfully, she desired to purchase platform furniture—specifically, a large, ornate ecclesiastical chair for me to sit in during the worship service. It would have stood out like a sore thumb against the modern appointments of our worship center. In this delicate situation, thankfully, the donor was open to a more appropriate gift that met the needs of the church and honored her husband. On rare occasions, gifts that do not match the church's mission or values should be declined if no common ground can be found—graciously, of course.

Can designated funds be redirected? Sometimes after a gift is given, needs and circumstances in the church change, rendering the gift inappropriate. Occasionally a church will raise funds for a project that becomes irrelevant. For example, suppose a church raised $2 million of a $5 million construction project and it becomes apparent that the additional funds are not going to be given or the church changes its focus and no longer needs the facility. A better problem would be if the church accidentally overfunded the project and raised $7 million for their $5 million project. In a related scenario, one church raised about $40,000 to resurface a parking lot, only to discover a looming roof failure that needed immediate repairs.

In most of the U.S., it's possible to redirect designated gifts. First, talk to the donors and obtain their permission to redirect the funds. In cases where the donors are unavailable or unknown, it might be appropriate for the church governing board or membership to vote on modifying use of the funds. It may be possible to present the circumstance to a civil judge for redirect. Obviously, these are awkward situations that anyone would prefer to avoid.

While legal or tax counsel should be sought for specific situations, you may be able to prevent problems by including contingency language in fund appeals, such as "In the unlikely event that this project is either overfunded or abandoned, the elder board will be authorized to use the funds in the most effective manner to accomplish the vision of the church." Donors and potential donors should be made aware of the disclosure. Such redirections of designated gifts should be rare so as not to diminish donor trust.

Handling Legal Aspects of Designated Giving

The legal side of designated giving is complicated, but a competent treasurer combined with a healthy annual audit is usually sufficient to keep funds in order. However, a Christian church needs to hold itself to a significantly higher standard than only that which is legal. When someone designates a gift to a church, he or she expects the gift to be used accordingly. It is immoral for the church to accept money designated for specific purposes and use it for general purposes. Such a practice will quickly erode the confidence that donors have in the financial integrity of the church.

There are painful cases where donors actually have brought legal action against the church on the basis of inappropriate use of designated funds. The courts yield mixed results in such cases. On the one hand, the donor made a charitable gift relinquishing all rights to the use of the money. On the other hand, the church may have established a trust relationship on the use of the funds. It is best for the kingdom of God if the church conducts itself in such a squeaky clean manner that these problems never arise. A designated gift should be used by a church accordingly.

> It is immoral for the church to accept money designated for specific purposes and use it for general purposes.

Heartfelt Generosity

Every donor has a different history and brings a special set of experiences to the offering plate. I recently dealt with a Christian who experienced a financial windfall. She wanted to make a significant gift and had already tithed to her local church. I simply asked her, "What is important to you?" She had lived modestly for her entire life but had experienced periods of poverty-level existence. During the tough years, she had dealt with poor water systems in her rural setting. She recalled times of shortage and times when water had to be boiled for safety. She decided to give toward providing clean, fresh water to a community anywhere in the world.

Donors' money tends to follow their hearts. It is wise for a church to diversify its appeals, because different donors respond differently to needs. Donors have many options. Unlike secular nonprofits, the church should provide an atmosphere that facilitates God's speaking directly to hearts, thereby stirring generosity!

By Mark Lail

GIFTS IN KIND: TOO BIG FOR THE OFFERING PLATE

The phone calls came almost back-to-back from a farmer and a pastor, each looking at a different side of the same situation. The farmer, who was nearing retirement, wanted to reduce the size of his livestock inventory and give some of the proceeds to his church. But selling his livestock would create an unpleasant tax situation. He asked if there was a way to avoid some taxes. The pastor said, "I have a farmer who wants to make a gift after the sale of his cattle, and I don't know how to help him." Both were delighted to hear that agricultural producers can sell their commodities, such as livestock, grain, or hay, as a gift without the proceeds being taxable income. The livestock proceeded through the normal marketing path. The farmer was able to deduct the cost of raising the cattle from his income—and the pastor was relieved that he would not need a cattle truck to pick up the gift!

Untapped Riches

Most local churches are geared to receive offerings as cash, electronic transfers, or checks. Because churches usually ask for money, donors tend to give in that way. However, most people own more nonliquid assets than cash. To address this disconnect, churches should learn to ask for noncash gifts. Many people will respond cheerfully.

Offering a treasured possession or the product of one's own work to God can be a happy experience. I once found a 14k gold ring at a yard sale for only 25 cents. For fun, during a sermon, I passed it down the pews and then gave it to the first woman whom it fit. She enjoyed wearing it for a few weeks, and then dropped it back into the offering plate. Through the next several months the ring had many owners, each of whom had the joy of wearing the ring but also the joy of giving it.

> Most people own more nonliquid assets than cash.

A man I once pastored had a nice riding lawn mower he used to mow his own lawn and often the church's, as well. When he bought a new one, he planned to give the old mower to his church. But as he considered God's blessings, he felt so grateful that he decided to keep the old mower for himself and gave the new mower to the church!

Gifts NOT to Accept

Some noncash gifts should not be accepted. As tempting as it sounds to receive a million dollars' worth of retail inventory, you should not accept a gift of cellphone cases designed for models that were popular three Christmases ago. Noncash gifts should only be accepted if they have value and are easily liquidated. The church has too many Kingdom priorities to get bogged down selling items with no value in yard sales and flea markets.

Explaining to motivated donors that their gifts would cause the church more difficulty than good requires a delicate conversation. Auctioneers say that the hardest aspect of their job is explaining to people that their possessions are not worth as much as they think they are. So remember, relationships rule with donors.

Noncash gifts should only be accepted if they have value and are easily liquidated. The church has too many Kingdom priorities to get bogged down selling items with no value in yard sales and flea markets.

Real Estate and Vehicles

Gifts of real estate can yield significant funds for ministry and provide tax savings for the donors. The criteria for accepting a gift of real estate is different than for other types of assets. You should ask the donor to provide an independent, qualified appraisal of the property in order for the gift to be tax deductible. And the church should determine whether the property is marketable, has a clear deed, is void of environmental problems, current on taxes, and has no mortgages or liens associated with it. Most churches should engage the assistance of professionals, such as foundations that are experienced with such gifts and are available to assist churches. These steps may seem intimidating, but the potential dollar value of such gifts significantly outweighs the costs.

Donated cars, boats, motor homes, or any vehicle with a title requires special substantiation. Substantiation is the evidence the donor provides to verify that the vehicle is indeed a gift. The church will need to follow the instructions from the Internal Revenue Service for Form 1098-C (irs.gov/instructions/i1098c/index.html). The procedure for substantiation and reporting is not complicated, but failure to give attention to the details may have unpleasant consequences for all parties involved.

Legal Details

Donors who give noncash donations relinquish all rights to the gift. There can be no strings attached. The privileges of ownership have been transferred to the church, which may use it or sell it at its own discretion.

The church's responsibility for substantiation of noncash gifts is different than for cash gifts. Follow the directives of Internal Revenue Service Publication 526 (irs.gov/pub/irs-pdf/p526.pdf). Although the details of these regulations are beyond the scope of this chapter, here are some basic principles:

- The limit of deductibility for noncash gifts is likely to be lower than for cash gifts.

- The burden of valuation for a noncash gift rests on the donor. The church should not provide a value or serve as appraiser. A contribution receipt should say something like "The donor contributed a box of office supplies" rather than "The donor gave $50 worth of office supplies."

- The larger the noncash gift, the greater the substantiation requirements. For larger gifts, a representative of the church will even need to acknowledge the gift by signing the donor's tax form.

Stock and Trusts

Donating an appreciated asset may provide a significant tax advantage to a donor. Giving company stock is simple for both the donor and the church. However, to realize any tax savings, the donor must actually give the stock, rather than sell it and donate the proceeds from the sale.

Often noncash gifts come to churches from charitable trusts. Because these tend to be quite sophisticated, most local churches should not attempt to administer a charitable trust. A professional organization such as a denominational or community foundation can simplify things for a church. Walter, a single, senior adult man wished to will his home to his church. Walter was concerned that his church would be saddled with preparing the home for sale, that the process of selling would be a hassle, and that the transfer of the property to the church would be a burden on his executor. An organization designed to assist in planned giving helped Walter establish a life estate trust. The property was transferred immediately, rather than at death, yet Walter retained the privilege of living in the home for as long as he needs it. In addition to receiving a tax deduction, Walter felt at peace knowing his home would avoid probate and the sale would be conducted by professionals. Once Walter graduates to heaven, the church will have very little to do other than receive the funds from the sale.

As you can see, noncash gifting converts to significant ministry resources. A donated coin collection or piece of art provides funds that help the church accomplish its mission. Churches that receive gifts that do not fit in an offering plate are the ones who ask for them. And because churches so often appeal for money, asking for noncash gifts can many times be more palatable. So ask away! You'll be planting seeds to provide for the church for many years to come.

By Mark Lail

DO'S & DON'TS OF CAPITAL CAMPAIGNS

First Church was healthy but lacked passion. The leadership team discerned that it was time to re-energize the congregation. They would challenge the people to reinvest themselves in the many effective things that were already happening and also commit themselves to renewed ministry in the community and around the world. The leaders laid out compelling plans that included physical expansion, new worship services, new campuses in new communities, investment in world missions, a community teen center, deeper partnerships with local nonprofits, and much more. They would need money, and lots of it, to implement their plans.

When they launched the "GO" capital campaign, they challenged and inspired their people to embrace the Great Commission in new and exciting ways, and the people responded passionately. Not only did they raise the largest amount of money in the history of the church but they also saw tremendous growth in attendance, faith decisions, and overall impact.

A capital campaign is an intense, focused fundraising effort that takes place over a specific period of time— usually two or three years. An ideal capital campaign is more about vision than it is about money. This is why many leaders have taken to calling them "vision campaigns" in recent years. These efforts can clarify and communicate the mission and vision of the ministry, while challenging the people to participate in what God is doing.

> An ideal capital campaign is more about vision than it is about money.

Capital campaigns differ from general giving in that the funds raised are set aside for specific projects that typically fall outside the scope of normal operational expenses. In the past, campaigns were almost strictly for building or remodeling projects and were known as building campaigns. But today a church might enter into a campaign for a number of reasons, a few of which might be:

- *Expansion:* This could involve land purchase, relocation, new construction, or remodeling.

- *Large initiatives:* This would include categories such as multi-site ministry, church planting, or missions.

- *Debt reduction:* People embrace this purpose more than they did in the past, and with today's low interest rates, it can be a great option.

- *Missions:* A 10 percent or more investment into missions is appealing to younger generations and reminds the church that it is always about ministry, not buildings.

Campaign Do's and Don'ts

A successful capital campaign requires a significant amount of time, energy, and resources. But when done properly, a campaign will not only raise a large amount of money for ministry, but it will deepen the spiritual vitality of a congregation and increase enthusiasm for the mission of the church. These benefits are evident in the following seven areas that require special attention when conducting your campaign (courtesy of Phil Ling, founder of The Giving Church consulting team, www.thegivingchurch.com[6]):

1. Vision

Do clearly communicate the purpose of the campaign and direction of the church.
Don't be fuzzy or vague! People don't give to what they don't understand.

2. Expectations

Do prepare well, and set goals that are attainable for your church.
Don't wing it. You need to know the overall health of your church.

3. Commitment

Do recognize that the campaign process must take top priority, so you will have to commit time and energy to it.

Don't allow the campaign to be buried under other initiatives.

4. Communication
Do tailor and target your message to reach the person in front of you.
Don't deliver the same generic speech to everyone.

5. Spiritual foundations
Do help people understand how the project will help reach people for Jesus.
Don't neglect the spiritual reasons behind what you are doing.

6. Patience
Do recognize that it takes six months to get people to the starting line, and then you have to follow through for two to three more years!
Don't approach your campaign with a short-term mentality.

7. Consistency
Do keep communicating the vision in new and creative ways.
Don't stop sharing the vision. Remember, vision leaks!

Done properly, a campaign will not only raise a large amount of money for ministry, but it will deepen the spiritual vitality of a congregation and increase enthusiasm for the mission of the church.

Timeline of a Typical Campaign

1. Assessment (one-month duration)

Before entering into a campaign, a church should undergo an in-depth analysis of its organizational health, financial giving potential, and overall readiness for a campaign.

2. Planning (two- to four-month duration)

- *Vision clarity:* The leaders of your church should be able to clearly articulate what the church is about; why the campaign is necessary; what is at stake if you don't act; and what God-honoring, Kingdom-building results will occur if you succeed.

- *Campaign branding:* The campaign theme will be developed and all print and media pieces produced.

- *Team preparation:* The most successful campaigns do a great job of distributing workload, connecting people personally to the vision, and creating ownership. For most, this will involve many volunteers at every stage of the campaign.

3. Leadership (one-month duration)

Senior leadership of the church will seek to have one-on-one and small-group gatherings with the stakeholders, influencers, and leaders in the church. This 20 to 25 percent of the church will be the ones who give as much as 70 percent of the total amount pledged.

4. Public (one-month duration)

Usually four Sunday morning worship services are dedicated to the campaign. The goal is to focus on the biblical basis for stewardship and giving while pointing people to the mission and vision of the church. To support this, people share stories with the congregation about the impact their church is already having.

5. Commitment (one-week duration)

On the final Sunday of the campaign, the entire faith family is asked to make a two- or three-year financial pledge. A brief follow-up invitation can be made the following Sunday for people who were absent on the commitment Sunday.

6. Giving (two- or three-year duration)

This phase will require extended and regular follow-up, communication, and evaluation.

One Fund: A New Twist?

In recent years, some churches have experienced success with an approach called "one fund." During a traditional campaign, congregation members are encouraged to make a pledge to the campaign that is over and above their regular giving to the church. The financial gifts made to the capital campaign are kept separate from the church general fund, and all the numbers, initiatives, and achievements are reported separately. During a one-fund approach, rather than encouraging members to go "above and beyond," the emphasis is on everyone simply "taking their next step." In this approach, there are not multiple funds. Instead, the general fund and the capital needs of the church are combined, and they are reported as one larger number that is all-inclusive of church needs for a specific period of time—most often two years.

The advantage to this approach seems to be the streamlining of vision casting and communication. Everything is about the *one* vision for ministry, and the people are simply challenged to make a two-year pledge to that goal. There have been some exciting results produced by one-fund campaigns, but it is still too early to predict the long-term viability of this option.

While some choose to go it alone, most churches would be wise to speak to a capital campaign consultant. Churches that work with professional consultants tend to raise more money and have a more positive experience while doing so. Not all consultants are created equal, however, so do your research; initial consultations should always be free.

Capital campaigns present complex but exciting opportunities for churches. They call for a lot of thought, prayer, discernment, time, and work. The rewards, though, can be more than worth the effort: wider participation, deeper stewardship, refreshed vision, and re-energized mission and ministry, all for the sake of God's kingdom and the world.

By Brian Walton

BUILDING PROJECTS

So you've decided to build! Here are ten signposts to help you navigate the often confusing terrain that comes with building projects.

1. **Do a gut check.** First, stop to reconsider and ask yourself some hard questions. Do you really need to build? Have you added worship services? Are you using all of your spaces creatively? Are your motives for building appropriate? Ray Bowman, author of *When Not to Build*, says churches are sometimes encouraged to "build too big, build too soon, or build the wrong kind of building."[7]

2. **Assemble a building team.** This team will lead your church through the process of designing and constructing your building. Team members should be personally selected by senior leadership. A larger, staff-led church will want the person who is normally responsible for facilities to lead this team. When choosing team members, it is imperative to have people who are:

   - sold out to the vision
   - mature in their faith

- willing to put their personal preferences aside
- capable of "playing well with others"
- wise and discerning
- knowledgeable about the ministries and priorities of the church

It is also helpful, of course, if they have construction-related knowledge, but it's not as important as many people believe. The most successful churches rely heavily on competent professionals from outside the church.

A word about the pastor: The senior pastor should have input at every stage of the project. But if the pastor becomes overly involved, his or her family life will suffer, the ministry focus of the church will waiver, and people will lose sight of the overarching vision.

3. **Determine the delivery method.** It's important to be familiar with construction delivery methods. Four of the most common are described below. Each method has numerous variations, and each one has advantages and disadvantages compared to the others.

- *Design–bid–build:* The church hires an architect to create detailed construction drawings. When the drawings are 100 percent complete, they are given to builders, who then submit fixed-price bids for construction. In this method, the architect and the builder work directly for the church but independently from each other. The upside of this approach is lower prices, as the church receives competitive bids for construction. The downside is that the contractor does not give early input into the design, and therefore, the church benefits less from his or her expertise as the drawings are being developed. This method often leads to building plans that have been created with little budget consideration. This is how churches end up with drawings for buildings that they cannot realistically afford to build. Costly change orders during construction are also commonplace with this approach.

- *Design–build:* Using this method, the role of the architect and builder are combined into a single entity, the design–build contractor. Many churches prefer this method for simplicity because they are dealing with a single point of contact. It is also desirable because it claims to provide the church with lower costs, a guaranteed price, and a faster overall process. However, because there is no third party representing the church during the process, the church loses direct control over some design and quality decisions.

- *Construction management:* The architect, the building contractor, and many of the subcontractors work directly for the church. The church functions as the general contractor but hires an independent construction manager to work directly for the church and oversee the entire process. The church pays the construction manager a set fee for his or her services but with no guaranteed maximum price. The final cost of the building is determined by the bids and performance of the independent contractors involved.

- *Integrated project delivery (IPD):* The newest delivery method is IPD. The church hires both an architect and a building contractor at the beginning of the design process. Both work for the church, and all three parties work collaboratively from the beginning. The builder is able to provide detailed cost analysis and feedback to the architect at strategic intervals during design, and both the builder and the architect are fully accountable to the church as the owner.

  One company that has pioneered this approach is Building God's Way. They claim that their version of IPD "deliver[s] quality buildings...at costs significantly lower than traditional construction averages" and "eliminates many of the pitfalls inherent to standard models."[8]

4. Hire outside experts. The delivery method chosen by the church will dictate which professionals they hire first. But successful churches know that they must involve outside experts early and often during the design and construction process.

5. Decide what to build. Utilize the outside experts to help you examine your total ministry program and determine exactly what you need. The architect will then create your conceptual drawings. These are not detailed construction plans, but floor plans, site plans, and perhaps concept drawings of what the outside of the building might look like.

6. Meet "the man." At this stage it's a good idea to pay an informal visit to local officials with your conceptual drawings in hand. Churches generally make a mistake when they try to "fly under the radar" of government agencies and community groups. Early in the design process, using guidance from the experts you've hired, find out what your civic and legal requirements might be. In many cases you will deal with a state building inspector. Locally, your project could be most affected by the building department, the planning and zoning office, the fire marshal, and even your neighborhood association.

7. Count the cost. Depending on the delivery method you've chosen, you should be able to come up with some reasonably accurate cost estimates with your conceptual drawings. This is another gut-check step. Can you still afford to build this building? Consider not only money but the time and energy capacity of your church members.

8. Secure funding. Few churches have the funds available to pay cash for expansion. Most will need to conduct a capital campaign and obtain a construction loan.

> For more details on fundraising campaigns, see the "Do's and Don'ts of Capital Campaigns" chapter in this book.

- *Campaign:* The numbers can vary widely, but a healthy church should think in terms of raising an additional one-and-a-half to two times their annual giving over the course of a three-year campaign.

- *Loans:* A construction loan is a short-term note that functions much like a line of credit. The church will make only interest payments during construction, and the payments are based only on the funds actually disbursed. After construction is complete, the loan is converted to permanent financing.

9. Obtain building plans. The architect will create detailed drawings for every aspect of the project. These will be the extensive plans that are used to construct your building. This process takes several months to complete, so you may want to "green light" the architect to get started on these drawings while you are working on your funding. Caution: Construction drawings are expensive. Do not proceed with these unless you are certain you will be able to secure the necessary funding.

10. Break ground. The church building team should continue to monitor the project, working with the experts involved to ensure a quality facility when complete.

Building projects are challenging. Successful churches work especially hard during these endeavors to cast the spiritual vision of the church and keep the focus on ministry impact—which is likely what created the need for the project in the first place. The result of prayerful discernment and careful planning will be continued or even greater effectiveness in ministry and will be well worth the cost.

By Brian Walton

HOW TO DO PORTABLE CHURCH

"Portable church" is hardly a new concept. Acts 2:46 mentions a large body of Jerusalem Christians coming together in the Temple's outer court as well as smaller meetings in houses (Acts 12:12). According to historian Everett Ferguson, churches across the Roman Empire must have met like this for at least several hundred years. Evidence from ancient Rome indicates that most churches in need of large spaces used warehouses or large apartments. It wasn't until after A.D. 313, when Christianity became a legally recognized religion, that congregations began to routinely purchase property and construct their own church buildings.[9]

Today, different challenges lead congregations to consider returning to our portable roots—namely, the escalating prices of real estate and construction. But these challenges have turned into opportunities for growth. Carey Nieuwhof, pastor of a large, multi-site portable church in Toronto, observes that unchurched people like attending a portable church because it doesn't feel like a traditional church.[10]

Nieuwhof's leadership team values the flexibility this strategy provides. A portable venue can be upsized, downsized, or relocated with relative ease. Nieuwhof acknowledges the hard work that comes with constantly setting up and tearing down but points to more than five years of evidence that the work is sustainable if it's well organized. Nieuwhof's church recently built a permanent structure as a hub for its portable churches, but it continues to plant portable sites and branches.

Grace Church in Erie, Pennsylvania, which began as a 130-year-old brick-and-mortar church, has found new life with the portable model. The church relocated its campus in 2007 but quickly discovered the church was growing at a rate that would require another costly building program. Instead, the church set a goal of launching multiple portable sites over the next five years. Derek Sanford, the lead pastor, noted that the portable model changed the culture of the church, since there are more opportunities for volunteers to get involved and to step into leadership roles.

So the portable model is attractive, whether you're a startup church or an established congregation, a church that meets in a single location or a multi-site. Here are some factors to consider before entering the world of portable church.

Choosing a Venue

One of the most important decisions to make is *where* you take your portable church. Ideally, you'll want to place your portable church in close proximity to where your launch team lives. Your church will grow primarily through word-of-mouth and personal invitations, so your church services should be held near where those relationships are forming.

Public schools are a popular choice for portable church because their auditoriums usually provide adequate stages, seating, sound, and lighting solutions. Other venues, such as a YMCA, require extensive setting up of chairs and equipment. Be sure to choose a site that is known by the community and is easily accessible.

When choosing a site, look not only at the worship space but the children's space, as well. Is there enough space for children to be comfortable? (Because of their energy levels and need to use their large motor skills, elementary children require more space than preschoolers.) Make sure you can limit access into your children's area in order to provide adequate security. Within the secure area, children should have easy access to water and bathrooms. Finally, is the children's area located where you can easily cart your equipment in and out each week? (See more on children's ministry below.)

Budget

A portable church allows a congregation to skip the expenses of purchasing land and paying for construction. However, there are considerable startup costs, whether you purchase entire packages from a portable church vendor (see the sidebar at the end of this chapter) or

> For more details on capital campaigns, see the "Do's and Don'ts of Capital Campaigns" chapter in this book.

assemble and organize everything yourself. Work with your ministry teams to estimate your launch costs and decide how your congregation will acquire those funds. Two primary options are obtaining a loan or having a capital campaign.

Data Management and Communication

Portable worship demands portable data management solutions for your children's security and attendance systems, volunteer management, and financial tracking. Consult with other portable churches to find out what web-based software solutions are working for them. Use services like Facebook private groups, Dropbox, and Google Docs to connect volunteers to each other and to share important files.

> For more details on choosing data management solutions, see the "Church Management Software" chapter in this book.

Marketing

Develop a plan to let your community know that you're launching. Send the newspaper a press release. In the months leading up to your launch, get involved in the community. Use its parades, fairs, and other events as platforms to let your neighbors know about your church. If your budget allows, consider a plan for direct mailing to your neighbors.

Children's Ministry

Being portable means that you'll be somewhat limited in toys and equipment for teaching children. If you are meeting in a school, you might have desks available that are the right size for elementary-age children. However, you may need to purchase plastic picnic tables from a toy store for your preschoolers. Puzzle-piece floor mats that you can take apart and reassemble each week will provide adequate cushioning for babies and preschoolers with emerging motor skills. Labeled tubs for each room can contain necessary supplies for that age group's needs.

Perhaps most important, you'll need to acquire a vibrant curriculum that sufficiently fills the time allotted to you. Coinciding with that, develop a system for providing snacks and supplies needed for that week's curriculum, which may change from week to week.

Worship

Depending on your venue, portable staging, backdrops, and chairs may need to be part of your worship setup. Attractive signage should also be considered; it can soften an institutional setting, shrink a big room, and provide direction to visitors.

Use durable yet lightweight sound equipment and possibly lighting that travels well. In addition, you need to decide where your musicians will rehearse each week. If they cannot use the same location where weekend services are held, consider asking a nearby church if you could borrow space in their church at some time when it's normally not being used by them. Some portable churches have their musicians arrive early on Sunday morning. They either have a full rehearsal or simply run through the songs once, assuming musicians practiced their parts on their own during the week.

Moving and Storing the Equipment

Your church will need to acquire a box truck or enclosed trailer large enough to accommodate all of the equipment and supplies you'll be using each week. Sound and music equipment will need sturdy travel cases. Almost everything else should be stored in clearly labeled stackable plastic tubs. Once you've mastered the art of perfectly packing your vehicle, take pictures so new volunteers can keep everything in order week after week.

You'll need to acquire a secure place to store your equipment vehicle during the week. Cold climates might require a heated space to protect the electronic equipment and any liquid supplies you have.

History, both ancient and modern, has demonstrated the value of portable church models. Following this model, whether by choice or by necessity, can be a means of God's blessings to the surrounding community and can bring spiritual vitality to your church.

There are numerous vendors dedicated to meeting these needs and more related to portable church. Here are a few to get you started:

- Church on Wheels—churchonwheels.com
- Portable Church Industries—portablechurch.com
- Church. in a Box—churchinaboxsolutions.com

By Larry Shallenberger

CHURCH MANAGEMENT SOFTWARE

Every day, a typical church juggles a nearly endless list of administrative tasks. How do you manage it all? Do you have separate documents containing lists of members, mailing labels, giving records, baptism records, and a directory? When you get a new address for someone, do you find yourself revising it in multiple lists?

You might need Church Management Software (ChMS). ChMS is specialized computer software that helps churches organize lists, records, and everyday tasks. This can be as simple as a Microsoft Access database or as sophisticated as a cloud-based application. Here are some guidelines for deciding what software might be a good fit for you.

Custom or Purchased Software?

One option is to ask a programmer in your church to write a database program. Having a volunteer create a custom solution has the benefits of working exactly the way you want, with lower startup costs. For example, I once set up an Access database to manage many of my church's daily tasks. The solution was adequate, and the reports exactly fit the needs of our church.

However, such solutions may have problems with support. For example, only the programmer knows how everything works. What happens if that person is unavailable at a crucial moment or permanently moves away? Custom programs can also quickly become obsolete. On the other hand, established ChMS vendors benefit from working with multiple churches, they have a team of programmers, and they offer customer support. In the end, the hidden costs in a build-your-own solution can be much higher than a purchased package.

Key Features of ChMS

Every provider offers different features; some of the more essential ones are described below. Extended or custom features can be found in the sidebar. You and your team will need to determine which features are crucial to your ministry.

Membership profiles: Membership profiles store basic information for each person in your church. They include contact information, names of family members, membership status, social media pages, and significant life events such as anniversaries, baptisms, and baby dedications. A good ChMS should be able to manage multiple addresses, phone numbers, and email addresses for each person. Profiles are the core of the system. Because all other features tie back to them,

Extended and Custom Features to Consider

- Accounting integration
- Attendance tracking
- Calendar
- Child check-in
- Donation management
- Emails to individuals/groups
- Event management
- Family records and profiles
- Groups
- Library management
- Member directory
- Member profiles
- Membership management
- Multi-site
- Newsletter
- Online giving
- Outreach and follow-up
- Pledge management
- Resource/facility management
- Text message service
- Volunteer management
- Worship planning

profiles must be as comprehensive and customizable as possible.

Donation management: Most churches send their donors annual or quarterly giving statements. Good systems should manage donor names, contact information, and giving records, including online contributions. Data entry needs to be accurate and easy, especially if your church uses volunteers to record and process this information.

Outreach and follow-up: What happens when someone visits for the first time? Do you send a letter, make a phone call, or visit their home? Do you track guest attendance? What happens on the second, third, and fourth visits? Do you know if someone has been gone multiple weeks in a row? No matter how you assimilate new people and care for current attendees, your ChMS needs to expedite the process and record what has happened. Check whether it will work with your current process. If not, consider adapting your process to fit the database solution. Both need to work hand-in-hand.

Attendance tracking/check-in: Knowing when people attend worship, Bible study classes, small groups, or other events can help measure how well connected they are to the church. Many churches have a secure check-in system for children; a good ChMS solution should offer efficient self-check-in procedures that also record attendance.

Group management: A group can be a Bible study group, a Sunday School class, worship team, small-group leaders, funeral dinner volunteers, or even Sunday morning worship attendees. A ChMS should be able to easily add names to groups, track participation, and create reports, including paper check-in sheets.

User-Friendly Software

User-friendliness is extremely important. If pastors, administrative staff, or volunteers are not comfortable, they will find another way to accomplish the task. Parishioners may also become users as they view and edit their own personal data. Choose a ChMS that suits the needs and skill level of those who will be using it.

Hosting Locally or in the Cloud?

Most traditional solutions are hosted locally, meaning the software/database resides on a church computer or server. Since the data is accessed only from a computer at church, security risks are minimal. For the same reason, though, availability may be limited. If the software is on a single computer, only one person at a time can use the program.

With cloud solutions, data is stored on a remote server and accessed via the Internet, making information more readily available. Pastors can obtain an address from their PC, Mac, mobile phone, or tablet in the office, at home, or in the car. Parts of the database can be opened up for parishioners to see and/or edit their information, view their giving records, or receive an electronic version of the church directory. Calendars and online giving can be linked and shared on a public website.

Popular Options

Below is a list of some popular church management software. This is not an exhaustive list or an endorsement for any particular system. The best choice will be what best fits your congregation.

- ACS Technologies—acstechnologies.com
- TouchPoint—touchpointsoftware.com
- Church Community Builder—ccbpress.com
- Fellowship One—fellowshipone.com
- ParishSOFT/Logos—parishsoft.com
- Servant Keeper—servantpc.com
- Shelby Church Management—shelbysystems.com

Costs of ChMS

You can pay for ChMS solutions in one of three ways. The first is a pay-per-member/record strategy. The price is determined by the number of individuals in your database. One caution: As your church grows and you add new people to the database, the cost will grow, as well.

The second strategy is the pay-per-attendee/active-member method. It doesn't matter how many records are in your database; you pay only for the records that are active. Being active is determined differently per vendor, but many are based on your average worship attendance.

The third, more traditional, strategy is to charge a license fee. This can be either an annual payment or a fee for initial purchase plus updates as they are added.

How to Evaluate Solutions

Choosing the right solution for your church will take time and patience. Here are some tips.

- Ask for help. There likely are people in your congregation who have experience with similar solutions in their workplaces. They can help you understand and spot helpful features. Talk to other churches of similar size to get their recommendations. Potential vendors can also provide clients you can contact. Ask what they like and don't like about their solution.

- Include end users in the selection process. Consult with the people who will be using the software. Their buy-in and knowledge of how things are currently done is essential to choosing the best solution.

- Research the options. Read and watch all you can. Many vendors have introductory videos available online. These videos will give the best description of the features and user-friendliness.

- Narrow your choices. Determine which features are essential to what you do now, which ones you may need for future tasks, and which features are unnecessary. Then select the two or three solutions that best fit your criteria.

- Once the finalists have been chosen, schedule vendor demonstrations. Ask lots of questions. If you don't fully understand how something works, ask them to show you again. Take your time. Be sure you are comfortable with the product and the presenter—this interaction may be a glimpse of that company's future support.

Conclusion

Church management software can greatly enhance your ministry through administrative efficiency, effective communication, congregational connectedness, improved assimilation, and the effective engagement of volunteers and donors. With some time and patience, the best solution for your ministry methodology can be found.

By Tom Barnes

ONLINE AND SOCIAL MEDIA PRESENCE

Pastor Brad noticed the emotional distance the moment he walked into the hospital room. Carrie, one of Brad's church members, remained seated next to her bedridden husband, Gary, who was still recovering from an unexpected heart attack. Carrie offered a cordial greeting but her body language indicated hurt. The Fergusons had been here for three days, and this was the first pastoral visit.

Brad apologized profusely. "I'm *so sorry* I'm just now getting here. I honestly didn't hear about you until today when someone in the church office said we should pray for you."

"I posted it online when it happened," Carrie countered. She stopped short of saying anything else, as if this was a valid point in itself.

Virtual Expectations

Not that long ago, society generally acknowledged that it took time to return phone calls or emails, especially if the respondent wasn't near a landline phone or personal computer. But now we're accustomed to instant access through texts, emails, direct messages, tagged posts, or cellphones. Not attending to someone in the virtual world can determine your relationship in the real world.

Providing virtual attention can be tricky when the technology changes so fast and everyone seems to have their favorite social media, especially younger generations. What apps should you use this week— Facebook? Instagram? Twitter?

> Not attending to someone in the virtual world can determine your relationship in the real world.

Online social connections have amplified expectations and dissolved personal boundaries. People in your congregation expect to access some version of you based on what they want out of the relationship. Consider these four categories of expectation:

- *Theologian:* People who feel stuck biblically or encounter curveball questions from friends tend to want perspective from someone who can competently address their inquiries.

- *Counselor:* Even the most grounded church members will have an occasional emotional or family crisis for which they'll want immediate help. Clinical counseling may seem too complicated or expensive when compared to a minister they already know and trust.

- *Mentor:* Because of either your position or your character, others likely look up to you. Some of them may approach you directly and ask you to mentor them. Others simply want to be close enough that they can observe how you live and lead.

- *Buddy:* Offers for friendship beyond your ministry role or title are usually well-intentioned, as individuals hope you'll feel you can "be yourself" with them. Other times a person wants this kind of relationship because they'd rather not think of your spiritual or leadership role at all.

Turning Stumbling Blocks Into Stepping Stones

These expectations cannot be dismissed, but they can be mediated through an effective online presence. The use of social media in ministry involves shared leadership and clear communication through various platforms.

Church website: Effective websites no longer require a skilled webmaster who has to build everything from the ground up. Now people without technical skills can use free or paid online services to create mobile-friendly sites simply by dragging and dropping data around. This opens the door for multiple users at your church to contribute fresh content on a regular basis, which

	Guests may want to see:	Members may want to see:
Theologian	Statement of faith; audio/video of sermons; personal information on the pastors	A tangible plan of where the leadership senses God wants to take the church; a forum to ask tough spiritual questions
Counselor	Recovery ministry; financial classes; marriage/divorce support	Direct emails and phone numbers to reach someone in a crisis; stories of how the church is reaching the community's needs
Mentor	Programs for children and youth; entry-level classes or groups to grow with God and others	Ideas on how to better live out and share their faith; a sign-up form for emails or text messages that will spur spiritual growth
Buddy	Actual pictures of the church versus stock photos; people who look/dress familiar; a link to social media pages; a promise that they can visit without being judged	An accurate calendar of events with any pertinent information (price, times, etc.)

ultimately makes Internet search engines favor your site over others.

Your website should serve in two different ways, depending on the type of user: 1) as a front door for guests; and 2) as a gathering place for your church members. Both groups will expect to find accurate and relevant information, which reflects the four categories of expectation, as depicted in the table on page 82.

Social media: Social media's greatest weakness is also its greatest strength: everything is public. Turning this to your advantage is as simple as getting as many people as possible to agree on what platform you'll use and how you'll use it.

- Think like a missionary. Ask the people in your church what forms of social media or electronic communication they prefer to use, and then join them there.

- Have an official account or page. Use it to spread news or announce events that others can link to and help promote.

- Cross pollinate. Upload church videos or sermons all in one place, but link to them on your social media platforms.

- Ask for interaction. Encourage your leaders and church members to comment on sermons, events, or your official blog posts.

- Create community. Create pages, groups, or circles within that network that link everyone together.

- Check in. Create a post or use whatever features that allow you to let others know where you're at, such as checking in during weekend services or letting others know you're available to connect at a local coffee shop.

- Spend money. Invest in whatever social media platform your local community generally uses to reach a specific demographic. For example, a promotion aimed at teenagers can either take them to your website's youth group page or a link to a special event. Steps on how to do this will differ from site to site, so look for "Help" or "Ads" info pages.

- Set measurable goals. Attempt to do something significant daily, weekly, monthly, and quarterly that will further your mission or the online community you're forming.

Keeping It Real

Hebrews 10:25 instructs us to "not neglect our meeting together, as some people do, but encourage one another." However active your church becomes technologically, continue to prioritize connecting in person. Your online and social media presence should *supplement* everyday relationships, not replace them. Virtual communication creates real emotions, some of which might arise from conclusions that are quite different from the original intent. Relationships will help you overcome this with trust instead of suspicion.

Your church will benefit from having policies on all of this to both guide and protect everyone involved. Consider what boundaries are necessary, such as interactions between adults and kids, as well as how you'll work out simple misunderstandings before they become worse. Every online post is public and influences how others think about God and church, so have open conversations about what a healthy online community feels like.

The downside to all of this is also its upside: while you will have to deal with people having greater proximity to your life, you'll also gain a greater proximity to their lives. Use this as an opportunity to enter into their journey as Jesus would, with radical hospitality, fearless conversation, genuine humility, and in anticipation of God's divine activity.[11]

By Tony Myles

ONLINE AND SOCIAL MEDIA PRESENCE

Endnotes

1. Nathaniel Tate, "The Church Administrator," *Ministry Today*, http://ministrytodaymag.com/ministry-today-archives/106-reviving-word/843-the-church-administrator#sthash.fSS23M2E.dpuf.

2. www.irs.gov/Charities-&-Non-Profits/Churches-&-Religious-Organizations

3. Mayo Clinic Staff, "Job burnout: How to spot it and take action," December 8, 2012, www.mayoclinic.org/healthy-living/adult-health/in-depth/burnout/art-20046642.

4. http://www.dol.gov/whd/regs/compliance/fairpay/fs17a_overview.pdf

5. Michael Gerber, *The E-myth: Why Most Small Businesses Don't Work and What to Do About It* (HarperBusiness, 1990).

6. Phil Ling, *Seven Ways to Kill a Capital Campaign* (Unpublished handbook for clients: 2010), 1-8. Used with permission.

7. Ray Bowman, *When Not to Build*, Expanded Edition (Grand Rapids, MI: Baker Books, 2000), 22.

8. www.bgwservices.com/Church_Construction_Delivery_Model/The_BGW_Difference.html.

9. Everett Ferguson, "Why and when did Christians start constructing special buildings for worship?", November 12, 2008, *Christianity Today*, www.christianitytoday.com/ch/asktheexpert/ask_churchbuildings.html.

10. Carey Nieuwhof, "Why Portable Church Should Be a Permanent Part of the Future," June 24, 2013, www.careynieuwhof.com/2013/06/why-portable-church-should-be-a-permanent-part-of-the-future/.

11. Thom and Joani Shultz, *Why Nobody Wants to Go to Church Anymore: And How 4 Acts of Love Will Make Your Church Irresistible* (Loveland, CO: Group Publishing, Inc., 2013).

PRACTICAL STUFF FOR PASTORS:
TAKING CARE OF BUSINESS